THE HERB BOOK

a guide to growing, preserving and cooking

Deborah Fowler and Sally Cuckson
Halzephron Herb Farm

Truran

First published in 2003 by Truran, Croft Prince, Mount Hawke, Truro,
Cornwall TR4 8EE
www.truranbooks.co.uk

Truran is an imprint of Truran Books Ltd

ISBN 1 85022 173 1

Cover photograph courtesy of Comstock from Cadmium Royalty Free

Printed and bound in Cornwall by R Booth Ltd,
Antron Hill, Mabe, Penryn, Cornwall TR10 9HH

CONTENTS

Dedicated to our children –

Tom, Michael, Charlie, Mark and Edita for all their dedicated and enthusiastic sampling over the years!

INTRODUCTION

Growing herbs, using herbs, preserving herbs is all part of everyday life at Halzephron. The gardens, the polytunnels, the storage areas, the workshops, the kitchens, the shop – and even our own home – smell of herbs throughout the year. Walking up the lane towards our house on a summer's evening, long before your reach it, you know you are approaching a herb farm.

Most of the staff who work at Halzephron have done so since the business began. I know I can speak for them, as well as for my family, in saying that in the last six years, the pleasure of working with these unique and wonderful plants has never dimmed. For me, there is no comparison between a bottle of Chanel No5 and the smell of a fresh basil leaf …. the basil wins every time – and it is a lot cheaper!

Most of the herbs we use today would have been familiar to people living in Europe three thousand years ago. Then, herbs were an integral and absolutely necessary part of day-to-day life, indeed, often life saving. Whereas in today's society, we tend to treat illness as something to be cured once it has struck, our forebears used herbs as a preventative medicine – a much more sensible approach.

Herbs in cooking have experienced a revival in this country since we all started travelling abroad, but herbs have always been part of the English culinary life. The recipes included in this book come from around the world. We have aimed to make them easy to follow, quick and simple to make and as far as possible, if not unique, then at least unusual. We have also tried to cater for all tastes – I do hope you enjoy them.

The information in this book on growing, cultivating and preserving herbs is based on our own personal experience at Halzephron. There is not a herb featured in this book we have not grown ourselves and we have learnt some very hard lessons along the way. I hope passing on this experience will prove useful. You may find my choice of herbs a little eccentric, but they do represent the most important ones, in my view, and are those most popular with our customers.

Deborah Fowler
Halzephron Herb Farm

BASIL

History

Basil is a native plant of India although today more people associate it with Italy and Italian dishes. In India, basil was held in such reverence that the Indians chose to swear their oaths in court upon the herb. Basil was said to have been found growing around Christ's tomb after the Resurrection. As a result some Greek Orthodox churches use basil to prepare holy water, and pots of basil are often placed at altar steps. Culpepper writes of basil in rather mysterious terms, saying that while it helps 'the deficiency of Venus in one kind, so it spoils all her actions in another. I dare write no more of it', making the herb sound like a rather dodgy love potion!

Cultivation

Tender annual, average growing height 45cm/18in.

There are many varieties of basil, details of which are listed on the following page. In general terms though, regardless of the type, I firmly believe that basil is an indoor plant. Many herb books talk of planting out basil in May, away from wind and frost. While you might find a very protected place in the garden or patio for your basil plant, you cannot protect it from the good old British summer and all those endless inches of rain! It is very easy to over water basil. It very quickly develops what is known as blackleg, where the stems become slimy and black, at which point, the best place for the plant is the dustbin. The time to water basil is when the plant is in full sunshine at high noon, exactly opposite to what you would do to most plants.

Preserving

Basil leaves can be dried or frozen. Basil is also wonderful preserved in olive oil and the resultant flavoured oil is marvellous in pastas and salads.

Mushroom and Sweet Basil Risotto
Serves 4

350g/12oz risotto rice
1 onion, finely chopped
1 large clove garlic, finely chopped
50g/2oz butter
2 tablespoons olive oil
150ml/¼pt dry white wine
900ml/½pt hot chicken stock (approx)
225g/8oz flat mushrooms, lightly sautéed
small packet dried porcini mushrooms –
(soaked as per packet instructions. Reserve soaking liquid)
2 tablespoons chopped fresh sweet basil
Parmesan cheese shavings to garnish
salt and freshly ground black pepper

Sweat the garlic and onion in the butter and olive oil until soft in a wide heavy pan. Add the rice and stir for 1–2 minutes to coat the grains with oil. Add the soaked porcini mushrooms, then start adding the stock about 150ml at a time. Add the liquid from the soaked porcini mushrooms and the white wine, and continue to add the stock until the rice is cooked (about 20–25 minutes). It may not be necessary to use all of the stock but the finished dish should be fairly moist.

About 5 minutes before the end of cooking add the sautéed flat mushrooms and half the basil. Check the seasoning. Garnish with Parmesan shavings and the remainder of the chopped basil.

BASIL

Basil is probably the most popular of all culinary herbs. It has a strong affinity with tomatoes, being wonderful in pasta sauces or simply with a tomato salad. Basil also has medicinal properties. For centuries, basil leaves have been used to draw the poison out of a venomous bite or sting, and basil is also good to use as a tea for indigestion, fevers, colds and flu. There are many types of basil, as follows:

Sweet Basil
This is the best known and most readily available basil, with large shiny leaves. It has a strong flavour and is excellent for cooking.

Greek Basil (Sometimes known as Basil Bush)
Greek Basil is the hardiest of all the basils and if you insist on growing your basil outside, this is the one which might survive. It is very compact with tiny leaves. The flavour is not as strong as sweet basil, but you will find it easier to grow.

Basil Neapolitana
This basil has large, crinkly leaves almost like lettuce. Its flavour is distinct from the other basils, much sharper. The lifespan of *Basil neapolitana* is very short and it does not stand up well to harvesting, but freezes well.

Basil Dark Opal
This is a pretty plant with purple leaves. The flavour is good, medium strength, but what is particularly nice about dark opal is its appearance. If you are planting a pot of basil, mix dark opal in with your green basil and the result is stunning.

Holy Basil
This is a small pretty plant with pink mauve flowers and deep purple stems. The scent and flavour is subtle and holy basil is wonderful in all types of oriental cooking.

Basils: Cinnamon, Lemon and Lime
These are three different, distinctive, dwarf basil plants whose flavour reflect their names. *Basil cinnamon* is wonderful in oriental cooking. *Basil lemon* and *lime* are great with chicken, fish and salads.

Curried Rice Noodles with Chicken

Serves 4–6

200g/7oz dried rice vermicelli
1½ tablespoons oil
1 tablespoon ready-made red curry paste
400g/14oz chicken thigh fillets, cut into fine strips
1–2 teaspoons chopped red chilli
2 tablespoons fish sauce
2 tablespoons lime juice
110g/4oz bean sprouts
75g/3oz chopped unsalted roasted peanuts (optional)
25g/1oz crisp fried onion
25g/1oz crisp fried garlic
25g/1oz fresh holy basil leaves

Cook the vermicelli in a pot of rapidly boiling water for 2 minutes. Drain and then toss with 2 teaspoons of the oil to prevent the strands from sticking together; set aside.

Heat the remaining oil in a wok. Add the curry paste and stir-fry for 1 minute or until fragrant. Add the chicken in batches and stir-fry for 2 minutes or until golden brown, finally returning all the chicken to the wok.

Add the chilli, fish sauce, lime juice and basil leaves; bring to the boil and simmer for 1 minute. Add the bean sprouts and vermicelli and toss well. Arrange the mixture on a serving plate and sprinkle with peanuts, onion and garlic. Serve immediately.

BAY

History

The bay tree is very special, for it was dedicated by the ancient Greeks to the god Apollo, the god of prophecy, poetry and healing. Apollo's prophecies were communicated through his priestess, Adelphi. She had many rituals, one of which was to eat a bay leaf before making her oracle. bay leaves are slightly narcotic in extremely large doses, so it is possible that she ate enough to induce a trance!

Cultivation

Evergreen tree, maximum growing height 7m/23ft.

It may be the result of living on top of a windy cliff, but I prefer bay trees planted in containers so that they can be moved indoors if the weather is particularly inclement. Once they are too big to bring inside, then I am prepared to admit they will probably survive outside! A bay tree likes a sunny spot, out of the wind, in a rich, moist, well-drained soil. Bay leaves are particularly susceptible to wind and frost. In addition to the bay tree we all know, there are two other main varieties – the golden bay which, as the name suggests, has golden leaves, a pretty tree which is slightly hardier than traditional bay, and willow leaf bay. Willow leaf bay is supposed to be less susceptible to winds and frost because the leaves are smaller. Our experience suggests this is not the case, and the leaves do not have nearly such a good flavour as traditional bay.

Preserving

You can dry bay leaves but they very rapidly lose their properties of flavour, aroma and colour. If you look after your tree, bay leaves can be picked all year round, thus avoiding the need to preserve them at all. Bay leaves are good in vinegar, giving the vinegar a distinctive and pleasant taste.

Potato, Bacon & Bay Leaf Gratin

Serves 4

450g/1lb potatoes, thinly sliced
1 onion, thinly sliced
110g/4oz bacon, diced (smoked or unsmoked according to taste)
2 bay leaves
150ml/¼pt milk
melted butter
salt and pepper

Gently fry the diced bacon in a little oil until it is slightly brown. Layer the sliced potatoes, onion and bacon in a gratin dish, seasoning each layer with salt and pepper. Push the bay leaves in amongst the potatoes. Add the milk and brush the top with melted butter. Cook in a preheated oven 180C/350F/gas mark 6 for approximately 1 hour until tender and brown on top.

Can be served with meat dishes or with a green salad.

BORAGE

History

Borage has long been associated with its ability to make people happy, and to give them courage. There is some medical evidence to support the latter. Borage is rich in calcium, potassium and mineral salts, which in turn stimulate the adrenal gland. Homer, on the other hand, saw it as a herb to be added to wine to induce 'absolute forgetfulness', which I suppose could make a person happy and inappropriately courageous! It may be this association between wine and borage, which today makes borage the favoured herb to add to a Pimms.

Cultivation

Hardy annual, height approximately 45cm/18in.
Borage is rather an untidy plant with prickly, hairy leaves and a rather straggled appearance, all of which is saved by beautiful blue flowers of a colour almost impossible to copy outside nature. It is easy to grow, preferring an open sunny position and a light dry well drained soil. While it is an annual, borage does self-seed very easily, and you need to give careful thought as to where you place it in the garden. Although not famed as a culinary herb, young leaves of borage can be cooked like spinach and are very tasty chopped into salads, yoghurts, cheeses or pasta sauces.

Preserving

You can dry both the flowers and the leaves of borage, though Culpepper maintains that once the herb is dried, however carefully, it has no medicinal qualities. His view is that borage leaves must be used fresh. As a medicinal herb, borage tea or tincture has been used for centuries to fight off colds, fevers and lung complaints. A poultice of leaves will reduce swelling and is good on bites and itchy, inflamed skin. Borage is also reputed to increase mothers' milk. As an added bonus, the flowers attract bees to your garden.

White Wine Cup

75ml/3floz sugar syrup (see recipe)
75ml/3floz lemon juice
250ml/9floz orange juice
4 tablespoons brandy
1 bottle semi-sweet white wine
3 long strips of cucumber peel
350ml/12floz sparkling mineral water
3–4 stalks borage, with flowers

Make the sugar syrup by putting 75g/3oz sugar in a small pan with 6 tablespoons water. Bring slowly to the boil, then simmer gently, stirring, until the sugar has dissolved. Cool, then pour into a glass jug and add the fruit juices, brandy and wine. Add the cucumber peel and chill in the refrigerator for 2–3 hours.

Shortly before serving, add the mineral water, plenty of ice and the borage.

CARAWAY

History

Caraway is a truly ancient herb with a very impressive past. It is mentioned in the Bible, in Shakespeare, it was found in Egyptian tombs and played an important part in Stone Age meals. Renowned for its seeds, used to flavour bread, cakes, pies and cheeses, this herb is reputed to give protection from witches, which might be useful! It also has been used through the centuries as a love potion, which sounds more fun. Culpepper, uncharacteristically more down to earth, recommends caraway as a cure for wind.

Cultivation

Hardy bi-annual, average growing height 60cm/24in in the second year. The caraway plant likes full sun and a rich soil. If both these factors are present then it is a surprisingly hardy plant, despite its fragile look. If you are a great bread maker but without a garden, caraway can be grown successfully inside on a sunny windowsill. The seed heads develop in late summer, assuming you sow in the spring, and should be harvested when the seeds are brown. Do not try to prolong the life of your plants after the second year – just dig them up and start again.

Preserving

Hang the seed heads somewhere dry over a container so that the seeds can drop into it. They are very small and narrow, only about a 5mm/¼in in length, so it is important you have a container to collect them in. When the seeds are collected, store them in a closed container somewhere dry and dark and their properties will be retained for at least a year. The leaves of caraway can be used to chop into soups and salads, but they do not freeze or dry very well. I would not recommend trying to preserve them.

Stir-Fried Cabbage with Caraway Seeds

Serves 4

1 medium green cabbage
2 tablespoons extra virgin olive oil
1 garlic clove, peeled and finely chopped (optional)
1 teaspoon caraway seeds
salt and pepper

Trim the outer leaves from the cabbage and shred the remaining cabbage finely. Heat oil in a heavy based saucepan and add the garlic. Moments later add the cabbage, caraway seeds and season with salt and pepper. Cook, stirring constantly, until just tender.

CATNIP/CATNEP/CAT MINT

History

It is believed that catnip derived its name from the Roman town of Nepiti. It is confusing for sometimes the plant is known as catnip, catnep or catmint, but catnip is the name most people favour. Catnip has a reputation both as a seasoning and a medicinal herb, but back in Roman times, it was the cannabis of the day. The leaves were dried and then smoked, producing a slightly hallucinogenic reaction generally believed to relieve the pressures of life!

Cultivation

Hardy herbaceous perennial, maximum growing height 1m/3ft.
Catnip is an easy plant to grow. It prefers sun or light shade and a well-drained soil, of not particularly good quality. Having established your catnip, taking cuttings is very easy. When set in a border, catnip is an attractive plant with purple, blue or white flowers which prove very attractive to bees....and CATS! Most cats go mad in the presence of catnip. They rub themselves along the leaves and roll in the plants, eat the young green leaves and shoots and generally cause absolute mayhem – albeit that you will have a very happy cat. However, some breeds appear to be immune to the charms of the plant. Of our three cats, only the farm moggy is interested. The two Burmese cats treat catnip with disdain, which I have since discovered is the experience of several of our customers.

Preserving

The only way to preserve catnip is to dry it. The best way is to cut long stems and dry the leaves on the stem, hanging the plant upside down in a cool dark place. The resultant dried leaves can then be stuffed into mouse shaped cloth to give as presents to your various cat friends. The smell of catnip also repels rats and it is well worth hanging the drying herb in places where you might have a rat problem, such as around the hen house or the dustbins.

I have included catnip in this book because it has proved such a popular herb with our customers over the years – both those who are cat lovers but also people who love the look of the plant and the fact that it so readily attracts bees to the garden.

Catnip does have culinary uses, going back centuries. Catnip leaves have been used to rub on red meat and the shoots and young leaves are very good in salads. Before china tea was introduced to the Western world, catnip was drunk as a delicate, fragrant tea without milk – it is very pleasant and refreshing. The tea should be made by adding a pint of boiling water to 40g/1½oz of dried catnip leaves, or 80g/3oz of fresh young catnip leaves.

Medicinally, catnip has a justifiable reputation for the relief of colds and fevers. Use the young leaves and flowering tops to make a strong tea. This will cause sweating which will reduce the body temperature and also induce sleep. A weak tea is also recommended for restless or hyperactive children and also children with colic or stomach upsets. Catnip is a very mild sedative and will do no one any harm if taken in moderation. It is very calming.

Culpepper swore by catnip. He was a great believer in an ointment made from the juice, which he maintained was good for both haemorrhoids and scabby heads. Pity the poor person who suffered from both of these at the same time! It is also reputed to have gynaecological uses – to cure the barren woman, and the nasty side effects of women's periods.

CHAMOMILE

History

Chamomile was well known to both the Greeks and the Egyptians. The Egyptians particularly valued it and dedicated the herb to the sun, worshipping it above all others for its healing properties. In this country, since Anglo Saxon times, chamomile has been valued for its medicinal uses and also as a lawn, used sometimes with, or instead of, grass. It is said that when Drake was playing bowls and waiting for his first sighting of the Spanish Armada, it was on the chamomile lawn that he played.

Cultivation

Hardy evergreen perennial, maximum growing height 20cm/8in.
Chamomile likes sunshine and a light well drained soil. In fact, chamomile thrives on a fairly sandy arid soil and certainly does not like permanently wet feet. There are two types of chamomile – the traditional one, which is used for medicinal and cosmetic purposes which has large cream flowers in abundance. The other type is lawn chamomile, which is grown quite specifically for that purpose. The flowers are daisy-like and not so profuse and the foliage is dwarf, not growing with the same abundance as that of traditional chamomile. Chamomile lawns are becoming increasingly popular. I think they are wonderful, particularly in the evening or after a little light rain, the smell is exquisite. If planting a chamomile lawn you should place your plants at 10–15cm/4–6in intervals and once established, do not be afraid to tread on the plants. Not only will they give off a beautiful fragrance, but it actually encourages their growth, hence the old proverb – 'like a chamomile bed, the more it is trodden the more it will spread'.

Preserving

Chamomile flowers and leaves should be dried, never frozen. They are easy to dry and maintain their properties well. Medicinally, chamomile has an established reputation for being anti-inflammatory, antispasmodic, a relaxant and anti-catarrhal. It is good for hay fever and asthma, and as an ointment, it is a wonderful healer.

CHAMOMILE

The only culinary use for chamomile is as a tea, which acts as a mild sedative and is generally calming. Chamomile tea is particularly good for restless children. Infuse both flowers and leaves with one pint of boiling water to 40g/1½oz of dried leaves and flowers, or 80g/3oz of fresh flowers and young leaves. Add a little honey for children. Chamomile tea is also very helpful for easing indigestion. I seem to remember it is what Mrs Rabbit gave Peter when he had a tummy ache from eating too many of Mr McGregor's lettuces! She knew a thing or two.

Chamomile has long been recognised as a cosmetic aid. Infuse the flowers for a facial steam to clear and whiten the skin. Add chamomile flowers to your bath to revive and refresh. Boil flowers for twenty minutes and use the water as a rinse to lighten and condition fair hair.

For household use, dried chamomile is excellent for pot pourri or for making herb pillows. A pillow made with a combination of dried hops and chamomile is very sleep inducing. If you have an abundance of chamomile, then jugs of fresh flowers and foliage around the house create a wonderful scent. For centuries chamomile was probably the most popular herb for strewing on floors to cover up the more pungent of medieval smells!

CHERVIL

History

Culpepper was somewhat dismissive of chervil – 'it is so harmless you can use it amiss'. This seems to be the herb's problem really – it is greatly underestimated. It has a delicate parsley flavour but there is a sharpness, too. The French value it and it is in fact one of the traditional 'fines herbes' and therefore considered indispensable to French cooking. Medicinally it has been associated for centuries with improving the appetite and expelling wind. It was also said that if chervil were drunk with wine, it would prevent the plague.

Cultivation

Hardy annual, maximum growing height 38cm/15in.
Chervil does not like hot conditions and full sun, when it quickly runs to seed. Light shade is the best place for your chervil plants and a light and well drained soil. Chervil self seeds very easily, so, once established, although the plant is an annual, you should have a constant supply. Harvest young leaves to chop into salads, soups, casseroles, fish and egg dishes.

Preserving

Chervil leaves can be frozen or dried, although if dried, I would recommend that they be used fairly quickly, as it is easy to lose their delicate flavour. Chervil is also excellent for flavouring vinegar. Raw chervil leaves are rich in vitamin C, carotene, iron and magnesium. Infuse in tea to stimulate digestion and alleviate circulation disorders, liver complaints and catarrh. A steamed infusion of the leaves or a facemask will maintain suppleness and discourage wrinkles. I admit I have yet to try it!

Roasted Cod with Herbs

Serves 4–6

50g/2oz flat leaf parsley
50g/2oz chervil
50g/2oz basil
2 tablespoons extra virgin olive oil
50g/2oz rough breadcrumbs
¼ chopped fresh red chilli, seeds removed (optional)
6 thick fillets of fresh cod
salt and freshly ground black pepper

Chop herbs finely and mix with olive oil, breadcrumbs, chilli, salt and pepper. Mix well. Spread paste on the top side of each fillet and chill for at least an hour. Place fillets on a pre-heated baking tray and bake at 200C/400F/gas mark 6 for 6–8 minutes, depending on thickness of fish. The fish should still be moist in the centre. Place fish under a preheated grill for 2 minutes until the topping forms a crust.

CHIVES

History

Chives were recorded four thousand years ago in China, and on his travels, Marco Polo discovered them there and reported on their virtues to the West. Culpepper did not seem to think much of them, particularly if they were eaten raw when he believed they would, 'Send up very hurtful vapours to the brain'

Cultivation

Hardy perennial, maximum growing height 1m/3ft.

Chives are very easy to grow. They prefer sun, but will survive partial shade and are not too fussy about the type of soil. They produce a most attractive pink/purple flower. As well as traditional chives, there are also garlic chives, sometimes known as the Chinese leek. Garlic chives have a strong garlic flavour and are excellent in stir-fries. When harvesting chives, leave about 5cm/2in of the stem for re-growth. Use them to garnish dishes, in dips, cheese, mayonnaise, soups and sauces. The flowers are good sprinkled on salads, they are both attractive and tasty.

Preserving

Chives can be dried or frozen, but I would recommend freezing. Garlic chives, in particular, are marvellous for adding to olive oil or vinegar, and if put in a sealed container, chives last very well in the fridge – certainly for at least a week – while still retaining their crispness. Both types of chives contain iron and vitamins and are a mild antibiotic. Sprinkle on food to stimulate appetite and promote digestion. They are also considered to be a mild laxative.

Twice Cooked Cheese and Chive Soufflés

Serves 6

For the ramekins:
butter
approx 2 tablespoons fine fresh breadcrumbs

For the soufflés:
50g/2oz butter
50g/2oz flour
300ml/½pt milk
175g/6oz grated Gruyere cheese
4 eggs, separated
2 tablespoons chives, chopped
300ml/½pt double cream
salt and freshly ground black pepper

Preheat oven to 200C/400F/gas mark 6. Generously butter the ramekins, add breadcrumbs and swirl around until all surfaces are coated. Put the butter, flour and milk (all cold) into a pan and bring slowly to the boil over low heat, stirring constantly with a wire whisk. The mixture will thicken as it comes to the boil. Reduce heat as low as possible and simmer for 10 minutes, stirring occasionally, until you have a smooth white sauce. Stir in half the cheese and season the mixture with salt and pepper. The sauce will be very thick. Remove the pan from the heat and allow the mixture to cool for about 5 minutes. Lightly whisk egg yolks and mix well into the sauce. Mix in the chopped chives. Whisk egg whites until stiff, but not dry, and fold them into the sauce mixture, beginning with a couple of tablespoons to slacken the mixture. Pour into the prepared ramekins and place in a bain-marie. Bake in the oven for 20–25 minutes until risen and firm. Leave to cool. They will immediately sink, but don't worry! Turn the soufflés out into buttered individual gratin dishes, or one large shallow dish. They can be kept in the fridge for up to 24 hours at this stage.

Heat the oven to 220C/425F/gas mark 7. Sprinkle the remaining cheese over the soufflés and pour over the cream. Arrange the dish or dishes on a baking sheet and bake for about 15 minutes, until bubbling and browned. Serve immediately.

COMFREY

History

Comfrey has a formidable reputation for healing but recent research has suggested that it should not be taken internally since it may cause liver disease. It did have a tremendous reputation for treating haemorrhaging and general bleeding, as well as its recognised benefits to sprains, bruises and broken bones. In fact, the old name for comfrey was knit-bone. In ointment form, which is perfectly safe, I always recommend that comfrey is an absolute essential piece of equipment for the mothers of sporty sons!

Cultivation

Hardy herbaceous perennial, maximum growing height 1.2m/4ft.
It is a messy plant, comfrey, which is not surprising as a member of the borage family. It likes damp, sunny spots where it will grow tall and fairly out of control. Once established, comfrey is a difficult plant to get rid of, so do position it carefully in your garden. Try and give it a low profile! The leaves of a comfrey plant are rich in protein and while I would not recommend comfrey to be taken internally as a regular medicine, certainly as a culinary herb, it can do you nothing but good, whether chopped into salads or soups or cooked as you would spinach. If you soak comfrey leaves in water for four weeks it provides a wonderful fertiliser for tomatoes and potato plants, owing to its high potash content.

Preserving

The leaves of comfrey are not really suitable for either freezing or drying and should be used fresh. Leaves added to your bath are very softening to the skin or added to a base oil, such as almond oil, they are very soothing for skin irritation. If you dig up the roots in late autumn they can be cleaned, chopped and dried and added to a base cream or oil for marvellous soothing and healing effects.

Comfrey Fritters

comfrey leaves
vegetable oil (for frying)
lime quarters (for garnish)

for the batter:
110g/4oz plain flour
pinch of salt
2 tablespoons sunflower oil
¼pt/150ml sparkling mineral water
1 egg white, stiffly beaten

First prepare the comfrey leaves. Trim off the stalks, clean the leaves carefully under cold running water and pat dry on kitchen roll.

Heat a large pan of clean vegetable oil until hot enough to brown a small cube of bread in 20 seconds. While the oil is heating, sift the flour with the salt into a large bowl, or food processor. Add the sunflower oil, beating all the time or processing, then start to add the sparkling water gradually, processing or beating constantly, stopping when the mixture has reached the consistency of fairly thick cream. Lastly, fold in the stiffly beaten egg white.

When the vegetable oil is at the right temperature, dip each leaf into the batter, shaking off the excess, then drop them into the hot oil a few at a time. Cook for about 3 minutes, or until golden brown, then lift out and drain on kitchen paper. Transfer to a warm dish whilst cooking the remaining leaves. Garnish with lime quarters and serve.

These fritters are particularly good served with a sauce of lightly minted yoghurt.

CORIANDER

History

Coriander has been cultivated as a medicinal and culinary herb for at least three thousand years. It was listed on 8th century Babylonian clay tablets, it is mentioned in *Tales of the Arabian Nights* and in the Bible. In ancient China, it was thought that anyone who ate coriander would enjoy immortality, and in the Middle Ages, across Europe, coriander was put into love potions as it was believed to be an aphrodisiac!

Cultivation

Hardy annual, maximum growing height 60cm/2ft.

Coriander is a very easy plant to grow. It is best to propagate the seeds indoors in February/March and plant outside in early May. Coriander enjoys full sun and a rich, light soil. Coriander is prized both for its leaves and for its seeds, and the trick is to harvest little and often. If you use your plant regularly it will become bushy and strong, if not, it will grow leggy and the leaves become yellow and unappetising. There is a new strain, which is now available in this country, called Vietnamese coriander. The smell, and taste, if anything, is a little stronger, and the great advantage of Vietnamese coriander is that it is perennial and almost impossible to kill off! Its leaves are long and pointed with an unusual horseshoe pattern on them, and cuttings are easy to take.

Preserving

It is quite impossible to freeze conventional coriander leaves. We have tried freezing them individually, mushing them up with a little olive oil, whatever you do, they turn to an awful green sludge when defrosted. The best way to preserve traditional coriander is to allow your plant to produce seeds, harvest the seeds, flash them in a medium oven for about three minutes then allow them to cool and place them in a sealed jar. They are wonderful in casseroles, curries, with rice, with steamed vegetables and quite honestly produce a far stronger and better flavour than coriander leaf. Not so with Vietnamese coriander which produces no seeds but the leaves freeze beautifully. Freeze them whole and break them up into small pieces, while they are still frozen.

Coriander and Chick Pea Casserole

Serves 4

2 x 400g/14oz tins chick peas
2 tablespoons sunflower oil
1 large onion, peeled and thinly sliced
2 large cloves of garlic, chopped
4 celery sticks, thinly sliced
2 medium carrots, thinly sliced
1 red pepper, thinly sliced
2 tablespoons ground coriander
1 x 400g/14oz tin chopped tomatoes
150ml/¼pt chicken stock
2 tablespoons chopped fresh coriander
salt and freshly ground black pepper

Heat the oil in a casserole and fry sliced onion, garlic, celery, carrots and red pepper over a moderate heat for a few minutes, stirring frequently. Add ground coriander and cook for about a minute. Add tomatoes, stock, chickpeas, half the chopped coriander, and seasoning. Bring to the boil and stir well. Cover and place in a preheated oven 120C/250F/gas mark 3 for about two hours. Taste and adjust seasoning. Garnish with remaining chopped coriander.

Serve with crusty bread.

DILL

History

Dill is very often associated these days with Scandanavia and fish dishes such as gravalax. In fact, the herb was known to the Ancient Eygptians, the Romans and the Greeks – the Greeks swore by it as a cure for hiccups! During the Middle Ages, it was prized as a herb for protection against witchcraft. 'Therewith her vervain and her dill, that hindereth Witches of their will'. Early settlers in North America took dill with them to church, where the seed became known as the 'meeting seed' because children were given dill seeds to chew during long sermons! Infused with wine, dill is reported to enhance passion. It is also known for its qualities of expelling wind!

Cultivation

Hardy annual, maximum growing height 60cm/2ft.
Dill is an easy plant to propagate and grow. It likes full sunshine and provided you do not put it outside too early, it is surprisingly hardy despite its fragile look. The biggest danger is the plant becoming leggy and going to seed too quickly. There is a particular type of dill known as dill dukat. If you can find dill dukat seeds, these are the best for leaf production. As with any herb plant, use it little and often and this will help new shoots to develop and make it a bushier plant. Dill can be grown indoors – in fact, it prospers well in a sunny window. Do not plant dill near fennel as they will cross-pollinate.

Preserving

You can dry or freeze the leaves. If you freeze them, freeze the leaves whole on the stems and then crush them while they are still frozen. Collect the seeds and dry them. They are great used like caraway seeds in cakes and breads, but also soups, fish dishes, pickles and chutneys. Add dill leaves to vinegar, with just a few seeds as well, or to mayonnaise which is lovely served with salmon. Dill really is a must for every herb garden.

Salmon Pasties with Dill and Watercress Sauce

Makes about 12; Serves 4–6

350g/12oz cooked flaked salmon
110g/4oz cooked long grain rice
2 tbs chopped spring onions
3 tablespoons chopped dill
40g/1½oz butter, melted
350g/12oz puff pastry

for watercress sauce:
1 bunch watercress
425ml/¾pt fish or chicken stock
40g/1½oz butter
2 tablespoons plain flour
300ml/½pt single cream
salt and black pepper

to glaze:
1 egg yolk, 1 tablespoon milk

Mix rice and fish together with the spring onions, dill, salt and pepper. Finally stir in the melted butter and set aside. Roll out the pastry quite thinly and cut it in circles about 7cm/3in across. Lay these on a floured surface and roll them out again separately, until you have very thin circles about 10cm/4in in diameter. Lay 1½ tablespoons of the salmon and rice filling on one half of each circle. Damp the edges of the pastry with water, all round the circle, and fold one half over the top of the other, pressing the edges together to seal and make a small slit in the centre of each. Beat the egg yolk with the milk and brush all over the pasties. Lay them on a greased baking sheet and bake in a pre-heated oven, 180C/350F/gas mark 4, for about 15–20 minutes until they are glazed golden brown.

Meanwhile pull the leaves off the watercress and set aside. Chop the stalks roughly and put in a pan with the stock. Bring to the boil slowly, cover and simmer for 20 minutes. Strain, then discard stalks and measure the stock. You should have about 300ml/½pt; if less, make up to this amount with extra stock or water. Melt the butter, add the flour and cook for 1 minute, stirring. Add the hot watercress stock and bring back to the boil. Simmer the mixture for another 3 minutes. Combine the cream with the watercress leaves in a liquidiser or food processor and add to the sauce. Reheat gently, and adding salt and pepper to taste. Serve the pasties soon after baking with the hot watercress sauce, as a light main dish with green salad, or as a substantial first course.

FENNEL

History

Fennel is mentioned in the papyrus writings of ancient Egypt and was one of the herbs used medicinally by Hippocrates. Greek athletes, training for the ancient Olympic Games, ate fennel to give them strength and to keep their weight down. It was brought to Northern Europe and was one of the nine sacred herbs of the Anglo-Saxons. In Tudor Britain, and in China, fennel has been used to neutralise snakebites. Charlemagne declared in 812AD that fennel was essential in every imperial garden.

Cultivation

Hardy herbaceous perennial, maximum growing height 2.1m/7ft.
Fennel is a very easygoing herb and extremely hard to kill off. It does prefer full sun and well-drained soil, but is pretty much prepared to grow anywhere. We have had the same fennel bed for about six years and apart from cropping it regularly and adding a bit of organic mulch in the winter, we do absolutely nothing. It self seeds, so that once your fennel bed is established, that's it. It is easy to confuse fennel with dill, fennel is a slightly coarser and much taller plant, and it is very important that since they are so similar, you do not plant them near one another because the seeds can cross-fertilise. Fennel can of course be grown for its 'bulbs', the swollen part of the root. If this is what you want, then clearly fennel becomes an annual and you should dig it up in the autumn to harvest the bulbs which are great cooked as a root vegetable or grated into salads.

Preserving

Fennel can be frozen or dried, but we have had more success in retaining quality by freezing. Like dill, freeze whole and crush while still frozen. Fennel seeds can be collected and dried and are delicious in sauces, fish dishes, bread and winter salads, adding a distinctive aniseed taste. Medicinally, fennel is well know as a means of easing indigestion, more recently it has proved to be an excellent remedy for a hangover!

Moroccan Lamb

Serves 4

700g/1½lb boneless lamb
seasoned flour
3 tablespoons olive oil
2 onions, sliced
2 green peppers, cut in strips
1 fennel, sliced
½ teaspoon ground ginger
600ml/1pt chicken or veal stock, heated
⅛ teaspoon saffron
110g/4oz dried apricots, chopped
1–2 tablespoons lemon juice
3 tablespoons chopped coriander
salt and black pepper

Cut the lamb into cubes and toss in the seasoned flour. Heat the oil in a sauté pan and brown the lamb, turning frequently. Remove from the pan and put in the prepared vegetables. Cook gently for 4–5 minutes, stirring often, until they are lightly coloured. Add the ginger towards the end, then replace the meat and pour on the heated stock, with the saffron, salt and pepper. Cover the pan and simmer gently for 1 hour, then add the chopped apricots and cook for a further 15 minutes until all is tender. Finally, stir in some lemon juice, to taste, and mix in half the chopped coriander. Turn into a serving dish and sprinkle over the remaining coriander.

Serve with boiled basmati rice and a green salad.

FEVERFEW

History

'Venus has commended this herb to succour her sisters, to be a general strengthener of their wombs, and to remedy such infirmities as a careless midwife has there caused.' So spoke Culpepper of this ancient herb. Although there are no culinary benefits to feverfew, I felt it right to include it in this book because its medicinal uses are so important and it is such an easy plant to grow. The herb's medicinal qualities are covered on the facing page, but suffice to say here, that going back through the centuries there can be few cottage gardens that did not have feverfew growing amongst the vegetables and flowers, much as today you might have a first aid kit in your kitchen.

Cultivation

Hardy perennial, maximum growing height 60cm/2ft.
Feverfew prefers a sunny spot and a well-drained soil. It is something of a scourge in the garden in as much as it does self seed very easily and you may well find it coming up all over the place, nonetheless, it is an attractive plant with daisy like flowers. You can use it as a border or planted close together as ground cover, all year round. Feverfew can be grown indoors in a cool place.

Preserving

Feverfew is best dried rather than frozen and both the leaves and flower can be infused to make a tea. The flower is good used in pot pourri, but do not include the leaf as the smell is not particularly pleasant. On the other hand, the leaf, when dried, and put in a muslin sachet is an excellent moth deterrent.

FEVERFEW

There are few of us in today's stressful world, who do not suffer from headaches, from time to time. There are many more unfortunates among us who suffer from recurring migraines. Feverfew's success in combating migraines and headaches is significant and has been the subject of scientific analysis and trials. In recent trials aimed at studying the performance of feverfew, 70% of patients experienced some improvement after eating a number of feverfew leaves every day, as compared with a 50% cure rate for the best drug available in the pharmaceutical market. Patients also found that there were other beneficial effects including more restful sleep and a degree of relief from arthritic pain.

Feverfew can be taken as a capsule, available from many health stores, but it is probably more effective to eat the fresh leaves. It has to be said that they taste filthy, but three to five fresh leaves a day, between bread or chopped into salad, can reduce migraines in sufferers. The point about feverfew is that it is not intended as a painkiller, something to knock you out when you already have the symptoms of a migraine or severe headache. The idea, if possible, is to start taking feverfew before the problem arises and continue it for several days after you feel better. However, one word of warning. In some people, the eating of feverfew leaves does produce mouth ulcers. It is therefore very important that when you have eaten your daily dose of leaves, you drink and gargle with some fresh water to make sure there is no residue of the herb left in your mouth.

As well as relieving arthritic and rheumatic pain, feverfew eases muscle spasms and acts as a tonic to encourage appetite. Centuries old texts list it as the herb to cure melancholy and vertigo, symptoms not unfamiliar to the modern day migraine sufferer.

Finally a few feverfew leaves 'the morning after', are an excellent hangover cure!

GARLIC

History

Garlic was eaten by the workers building the pyramids as a protection against illness. It is said the Holy Roman Empire was founded on garlic as Roman soldiers on long marches were fed a daily ration of it. The explorer Marco Polo reported garlic's culinary virtues to the West. The grandfather of the future Henri IV of France rubbed the new-born baby's lips with garlic and made him swallow a few drops of wine. This was to protect him from evil and to make sure that he could hold his drink! We all know it is believed in Eastern Europe that hanging garlic round your neck or your door deters vampires; in Sweden it is the trolls who are the evil threat to be kept away by this practice.

Cultivation

Hardy perennial, maximum growing height 20cm–1m/8in–3ft.
Of course, garlic is very rarely a perennial because we mostly dig it up for the cloves! Left to its own devices it would go on and on, producing white or pink flowers. It is recommended that if you are growing garlic on an annual basis that you should find a new spot for it each year. Planting garlic in the same place twice produces a very poor second crop. The cloves can be planted in spring or autumn in a damp rich soil. Remove flowers for a better flavour.

Preserving

Garlic can be frozen, if peeled and chopped and combined with a drop of oil before freezing. Garlic bulbs cannot be dried, they simply dry out. Garlic can also be preserved by placing it in olive oil or vinegar but it is best to roast the garlic a little first, for about ten minutes in a medium oven. Garlic has a well-known reputation for reducing blood cholesterol levels and lowering the chance of a heart attack. It is an important herb for circulation and increases blood thinning. Used externally, as an ointment, garlic is an anti-fungal and antiseptic. Above all, it is a great food enhancer!

Georgia Chicken

A great favourite with children
Serves 4–6

4–6 chicken pieces
110g/4oz melted butter
4 packets of crushed plain crisps
25g/1oz grated Parmesan cheese
2 tablespoons chopped fresh parsley
1 clove garlic, chopped

Combine crisps, Parmesan cheese, parsley and garlic in a bowl. Add salt and pepper to taste. Dip chicken pieces in melted butter, then roll in the crumb mixture until well coated.

Cook on a baking tray in a fairly hot oven 190C/375F/ gas mark 5 for approximately 25 minutes until crisp and brown.

Serve with French fries and salad.

HORSERADISH

History

Originally, horseradish was a cultivated plant used mainly as a medicinal herb. The juice from the boiled root was drunk as an effective cure for scurvy. It was also given to children to kill worms, and had a reputation for easing sciatica. By the late sixteenth century, it had developed a reputation as a flavouring herb and both the Germans and the Danes used it to make a fish sauce. Somewhere around the mid-sixteen hundreds, the recipe for horseradish sauce spread to Britain, and ever since it has been associated with roast beef.

Cultivation

Hardy perennial, maximum growing height 1m/3ft.

Horseradish likes a moist soil and can be grown in sun or partial shade and is normally a very easy plant to grow. We always find we have a problem with snails and horseradish. The leaves have quite a strong flavour and one would not have thought they would appeal to a snail, but they most certainly do. Although a perennial, horseradish is normally grown for its root and so in autumn should be dug up ready for use.

Preserving

You can store the whole roots in sand or slice and grate the root, either putting it straight into a sauce or drying it. You can also preserve the root by washing it carefully and placing it in white wine vinegar. As well as making traditional horseradish sauce, horseradish is lovely grated into coleslaw or dips, into mayonnaise or cream cheese. If you make an infusion from the root by simmering it in milk, the resultant mixture is said to improve skin clarity and mixed with a little white vinegar, will lighten freckles. This is for external use, I hasten to add. I cannot imagine horseradish milk would be very tasty!

A useful hardy addition to the garden – just watch out for those snails!

Bloody Mary

1.2 kg/2½lb (ripe or overripe red tomatoes
35g/1½oz coriander, washed well
small sprigs of thyme and parsley
20g /¾oz fresh horseradish root, peeled and chopped small
juice of 2 lemons and 2 limes
1 teaspoon salt
1 teaspoon caster sugar
2 cloves garlic, peeled
1 small red or green chilli

To serve:
vodka
sea salt
lime slices
celery sticks

Puree all ingredients in a liquidiser or food processor until smooth. Pass through a sieve, pushing the solids through with the back of a ladle. Adjust the seasoning to taste. Chill and serve in tall glasses, laced with vodka, sprinkled with sea salt, with a lime slice and celery stick in each glass. It is wonderful!

Horseradish Butter (To use on grilled steaks, etc)

225g/8oz butter, softened
110g/4oz grated horseradish
2 tablespoons lemon juice

Cream the butter in a food processor, adding the horseradish and lemon juice. Form into a roll, wrap in tinfoil and chill until needed. Can be frozen.

HYSSOP

History

Hyssop is an ancient herb known both to the Greeks and the Romans. It also has Biblical connections. Hyssop was believed to help lepers. 'Purge me with hyssop, and I shall be clean.' (Psalm 51, Verse 7). It was used to flavour wine, certainly by the Romans, and is thought to have influenced the Benedictine monks for use in flavouring their liqueurs. Culpepper thought hyssop was a great help in the aftermath of liver problems. 'It amends and cherishes the native colour of the body spoiled by the yellow fever.'

Cultivation

Hardy semi-evergreen perennial, maximum growing height 1.2m/4ft.
Hyssop comes in three colours – pink, purplish blue and white, all are very pretty flowers, easy to propagate and grow. They like full sun and a light well drained soil. Hyssop hedges are ideal for borders and knot gardens. If you grow hyssop near cabbages, it will lure away the cabbage white butterflies and if you have vines, plant hyssop nearby and it will increase the yield. To maintain your hyssop plants, cut them well back in autumn. Hyssop can be grown indoors.

Preserving

You can dry both the young leaves and the flower tops. The flowering tops can be infused as a tea, which is helpful for throat complaints and bronchial catarrh. Both leaves and flowers are excellent in pot pourri and a poultice of leaves is said to heal wounds and bruises. The fresh flowers can be used for tossing in salads and the leaves for rubbing on the skins of meats and fish, or chopping into rich stews, pates, soups or pies. Small amounts of the leaf aid digestion of fatty foods and fish.

Chicken Breasts with Calvados

Serves 4

4 chicken breasts
25g/1oz butter
1½ tablespoons olive oil
1 small onion, finely chopped
6 tablespoons Calvados
6 tablespoons chicken stock, heated
2 sprigs hyssop
1½ tablespoons chopped thyme
4 tablespoons crème fraiche
salt and freshly ground black pepper

Heat the butter and oil in a sauté pan and cook the chopped onion until it starts to soften. Add the chicken breasts and brown on each side. Pour the Calvados into a ladle and warm over a low heat, then set light to it and pour it, flaming, over the chicken breasts. Tilt the pan from side to side, and spoon the spirit over the chicken. When the flames have died down, add the heated stock and the hyssop and sprinkle with chopped thyme. Season with salt and pepper. Cover the pan and cook gently for 20 minutes or until cooked through.

Lift the chicken breasts onto a serving dish, then add the crème fraiche to the pan and warm through. Adjust the seasoning then pour the sauce over and around the chicken breasts.

LAVENDER

History

The fresh clean scent of lavender has been admired since Greek and Roman times when they used lavender as a bath water additive. Lavender was also used for strewing on the floor, in linen and generally around the household to disguise the very dodgy plumbing of earlier times. Indeed, the Latin 'lavary' means to wash. Generally, lavender is most associated with perfumes and the cosmetic industry but it is not without its medicinal virtues as well. Culpepper described it as a herb which 'Strengthens the stomach, and frees the liver and spleen from obstructions'. It is generally recognised by herbalists as a mild anti-depressant and is thought to be a general aid to problems of the brain, from headaches to apoplexy, convulsions and fainting. The story is told that the glovers of Grasse used lavender oil to scent their leather and that the plague passed them by. This encouraged the belief that people should carry lavender to ward off pestilence.

Cultivation

Hardy evergreen shrub, maximum growing height 45cm–1m/18in–3ft.
Lavender thrives on the dry sandy hillsides of Southern Europe with plenty of hot sunshine. It is therefore hardly surprising that it is difficult to grow lavender successfully in England where the soil tends to be heavy and wet. The place where you put your lavender should be sunny and open because it is very susceptible to fungus. While you may not be able to achieve a sandy soil, at least make sure it is well drained. Having secured the right soil and location, lavender essentially looks after itself and of course is wonderful for borders, knot gardens or just as a fragrant clump somewhere in your garden.

Preserving

Lavender should be dried. Cut the stems when the lavender has flowered and either bunch and hang them up to dry, or lay them in open trays.

Lavender Shortbread

1 teaspoon finely chopped lavender blossoms
110g/4oz caster sugar or lavender sugar (see below)
200g/7oz unsalted butter
300g/11oz plain flour
pinch of salt
2 drops of vanilla essence

Mix the lavender with the sugar (or lavender sugar, if using) then lightly cream it with the butter and vanilla essence. Sieve the flour with the salt and mix together with the creamed butter and sugar to make a soft dough. Chill for approximately 1 hour.

Preheat oven to 160C/325F/gas mark 3. Roll the dough to approximately 5mm thick and cut into rounds with a biscuit cutter. Place on a baking sheet, sprinkle with a little caster sugar and bake for 15–20 minutes or until pale golden. They will become crisp on cooling.

Lavender Sugar

Place 8–12 lavender blossoms in a jar of caster sugar and leave for 2 weeks.

LAVENDER

There are a number of different lavenders, brief details of which are as follows:

French Lavender
This is probably the best known of the lavenders. It is half-hardy with purple flowers and grey/green leaves. The scent is very pungent and therefore is the lavender most used by the cosmetic industry.

Lavender Vera
This also has purple flowers but the leaves are tiny and silver. It is a Dutch lavender by origin, small and relatively hardy.

Hidcote Lavender
This is a small plant with dark purple flowers and small silver leaves. It is slow to grow, but it is one of the hardiest.

Loddon Pink
This lavender has a very pretty pale pink flower and the chief advantage of *Loddon Pink* is that it is lovely to mix with other lavenders in your garden to provide a colour contrast. Faint scent.

Folgate
This is a small lavender with particularly rich purple/blue flowers and narrow grey/green leaves. Like most of the small lavenders it is fairly hardy.

Nana Alba
This lavender has white flowers and silver/grey foliage. It is a very small plant, growing no more than 30cm/12in in height, without a strong scent.

Munstead
This is another smallish lavender with purple flowers and rather more greenish leaves than most lavender. It flowers early and is unlikely to grow above a height of 45cm/18in.

Sawyer's Hybrid
This is a useful, relatively new, lavender with silver leaves and large purple flowers. The chief advantage of *Sawyer's Hybrid* is that it is a strong plant and probably the hardiest of all lavenders.

There are one or two hybrid species but these are the main lavender for you to consider. For best results, choose several varieties and see which does best in your garden. Too many varieties will look a mess – aim for two or three.

Lavender Ice Cream

Serves 4–6

300ml/½pt milk
20 lavender flowers
4 egg yolks
25g/1oz caster sugar
4 tablespoons clear honey
300ml/½pt double cream, lightly whipped

Put the milk in a pan with the lavender flowers. Bring slowly to the boil then remove from the heat and cover with a lid. Leave to infuse for 20–30 minutes, then strain out the lavender and discard.

Put the egg yolks into a bowl and beat with an electric beater, adding the sugar gradually. Continue to beat for 2–3 minutes, then reheat the lavender-flavoured milk. Next, put the bowl over a saucepan of barely simmering water. Start to beat the egg yolks again and as the milk nears boiling point, pour it slowly on to the eggs, beating continuously. Using a wooden spoon now instead of an electric beater, stir constantly until the custard has thickened just enough to coat the back of the wooden spoon.

Lift the bowl off the saucepan and stand it in a sink half full of cold water. Stir now and then as the custard cools to room temperature, to prevent a skin forming.

When the custard has cooled to room temperature, stir in the honey then fold in the lightly whipped cream and pour into an ice-cream machine and freeze, following the maker's instructions. Alternatively, pour the mixture into a container and place in the freezer to freeze.

LEMON BALM

History

Lemon Balm is a much-loved herb, sacred to the temple of Diana, and used medicinally for over two thousand years, especially by the Greeks. Lemon balm has been described as the 'elixir of life' and as 'a heart's delight'. The London Dispensary, a medical journal, stated in 1696 that 'Balm given every morning will renew youth, strengthen the brain and relieve languishing nature'. This suggests that most of us could do with a tincture of lemon balm! It is claimed that in the thirteenth century Llewyllen, Prince of Glamorgan lived to be 108 because of his regular morning tea of lemon balm. John Hussey of Sydenham, lived to be 116 after fifty years of breakfasting on lemon balm tea with honey. John Gerrard claimed that 'balm drunk in wine is good against the bitings of venomous beasts, comforts the heart, and drivest away all melancholy and sadness.' Lemon balm is certainly a herb that suggests cheerfulness and is used today by modern herbalists to counter depression.

Cultivation

Hardy herbaceous perennial, maximum growing height 1m/3ft.
Lemon balm is a very easy plant to grow. It likes a moist soil but is happy in sun or light shade. My own experience is that it is very important to use lemon balm regularly, otherwise it tends to go woody and brown underneath the new leaves, rather like mint is inclined to do. Pick leaves any time but handle carefully, as they do bruise easily.

Preserving

Lemon balm is best dried rather than frozen. You can add fresh leaves to vinegar or dry the leaves to make tea (to ensure you receive your telegram from the Queen!). Lemon balm is lovely in pot pourri and has a wide range of culinary uses in sauces, mayonnaise, and custards, wine cups, with poultry, or pork in particular and, of course, with fish.

Chicken and Orange Pot Roast

Serves 4

1.5kg/3½lb chicken
juice of 2 oranges
1 cup of fresh lemon balm
4 large basil leaves
salt and black pepper
300ml/½pt chicken stock

Put a little olive oil in a flameproof casserole dish and heat. Place the whole chicken in and let it brown all over, turning regularly. Add the lemon balm and pour the orange juice and stock over the chicken, add salt, pepper and basil. Cover and cook in a moderate oven for 1½ hours 150C/300F/gas mark 2.

When cooked, remove bird from casserole and carve. Arrange pieces on a hot serving dish. Strain cooking juices and pour over the chicken pieces.

Keep back a little uncooked basil and lemon balm to garnish.

Serve with noodles and a green salad.

LEMON VERBENA

History

Lemon verbena is a native of South America. The Spanish brought it to Europe in the seventeenth century and grew it as a plant to perfume oil. Medicinally, lemon verbena is good for coughs, colds, wheezing and shortness of breath and a tea, made from the leaves, will not only help these symptoms but is also a mild sedative. Culpepper had an interesting view on the use of verbena, 'use with lard, it helps swellings and pains in the secret parts'!

Cultivation

Half-hardy shrub, maximum growing height 1.2m/4ft – although in hot climates it can grow to 4.5m/15ft.
I love lemon verbena, its fresh, sharp lemon smell so distinctive. However, we struggle to grow it because it is a plant, which hates strong winds and hankers after a life in the sun. So plant it in full sun, in a well-drained soil, remembering its origins are South America, so a heavy, rich soil is quite wrong. In winter it will survive if you cut it right back and put a thick mulch around the pruned plant.

Preserving

This is a plant that you should dry rather than freeze. The leaves can be picked at any time, but they are at their very best just when the flowers begin to bloom. You can use the leaves as described for a herb tea or to flavour oil or vinegar. They can be used in drinks, puddings, jellies and ice cream. Traditionally, lemon verbena has often been placed in finger bowls. Because of the plant's strong fragrance the dried leaf is ideal in pot pourri and herb pillows, you can infuse it into candle wax. If we have a surplus of lemon verbena, I simply use it as cut flowers, which gives the whole house a beautiful lemony smell.

Apricot Clafoutis

Serves 4–6

450g/1lb ripe apricots
25g/1oz butter
75g/3oz sugar
3 tablespoons brandy or dark rum
1 tablespoon finely chopped lemon verbena
250ml/9fl oz single cream or milk
3 eggs
60g/2½oz plain flour, sifted
icing sugar to decorate

Cut the apricots in half and remove the stones. Heat the butter in a large frying pan and cook the fruit lightly with 3 tablespoons of the sugar for 10 minutes. The apricots should retain their shape. Remove from the heat, add the brandy and the lemon verbena and leave to soak for 30 minutes. Heat the oven to 200C/400F/gas mark 6. Transfer the apricots, cut side uppermost, to a shallow 1–1½ litre (1¾–2½ pint) ovenproof dish.

Blend the cream, remaining sugar, eggs, flour and juices from the fruit at high speed in a food processor or blender. Pour over the fruit and bake for 30–35 minutes until the clafoutis is puffed up and lightly browned.

Serve warm (rather than hot) sprinkled with icing sugar.

LOVAGE

History

Lovage has been around in Europe for centuries, best known in earlier times for its medicinal properties. It was originally a native of the mountain districts of the Mediterranean, but has travelled to these shores very well and seems perfectly satisfied with our weird climate. Culpepper maintained that lovage leaves, 'bruised and fried in hogs lard and laid hot to any blotch or boil will quickly break it'. Lovage is generally held to be excellent for detoxing the system. Using the leaf and the root make an infusion of tea which will generally help to detox the system, including reducing water retention and easing indigestion. It also has a formidable reputation for helping throat infections, particularly quinsy. Rather quaintly, in the sixteenth and seventeenth century, lovage leaves used to be laid in the shoes of guests, overnight in coaching inns up and down the country, in order to revive the weary traveller.

Cultivation

Hardy herbaceous perennial, maximum growing height 2.1m/7ft.
Lovage is an easy plant to grow in almost any part of the garden and in any circumstances. It does prefer full sun and rich moist soil but this is a plant, which is seriously difficult to kill.

Preserving

The leaves can be frozen or dried, you can also dry the seeds and the roots if you are wishing to make a tea. For maximum benefit from the roots dig up only second or third year roots and do so before flowering. The seeds can be added to liqueurs, breads, pastries or sprinkled on salads, rice or steamed vegetables. Lovage soup is particularly delicious and fresh or dried leaves can be added to stews and casseroles, and the young leaves to salads. A truly versatile herb.

Braised Celery with Lovage

Serves 4

3 heads celery, trimmed and halved
50g/2oz butter
425ml/¾pt chicken or vegetable stock
2 tablespoons lemon juice
1½ tablespoons chopped lovage
100ml/3½fl oz soured cream or crème fraiche
grated Parmesan to serve
salt and freshly ground black pepper

Blanch the celery for 5 minutes in boiling water, then drain. Rub a heavy casserole with some of the butter and arrange the celery in one layer if possible. Dot with the remaining butter and pour over 300ml/½pt of the heated stock, adding the lemon juice, chopped lovage, salt and pepper. Cover and cook gently over a very low heat for approximately 1 hour until the celery is tender. Half way through cooking, turn the celery pieces and add more stock if required. When the celery is tender, transfer to a heatproof dish. Mix the juices with the soured cream or crème fraiche, check the seasoning, then pour over the celery.

Sprinkle with grated Parmesan and brown under a preheated grill.

MARIGOLD

History

This cheerful herb probably came originally from India, where it was considered to be sacred and used to decorate temple altars. The Ancient Greeks also valued marigold as a rejuvenating herb. Despite its climatic origins, marigolds have settled in this country very well and it is hard to imagine a traditional cottage garden without them. The flowers are best known for the garnishing of many culinary dishes down the centuries, but less well known is the fact that the leaves and flowers are soothing, healing and antiseptic. In the American Civil War, doctors on the battlefield used the leaves of marigold to treat open wounds.

Cultivation

Hardy annual, maximum growing height 50cm/20in.
Marigolds will grow in any soil, but they do like a sunny position. One of the many attractive features of the marigold plant is that it will continually flower throughout the summer, but only if you deadhead. Many people use marigold for borders. I prefer them dotted about in clumps. Because of their high colour, they do attract a variety of pests to them and we find they have been very useful in our herb gardens for keeping the creepy-crawlies away from our herbs.

Preserving

The only part of the marigold plant worth preserving are the flowers and these cannot be frozen, only dried. Do dry the petals at a low temperature otherwise they will lose their colour. The flowers dried or fresh can be added to creams and baths for healing and softening the skin. The flowers, again dried or fresh, can be infused to produce a tea which aids digestion and bile production in the liver, which is very useful to anyone with a drinking problem. Fresh flowers are lovely as a garnish, you can also sprinkle them into salads or stews, yoghurt, butter, cakes and rice. The dried flower petals are obviously very decorative in pot pourri, although they contribute nothing to the scent.

Marigold Tart

Serves 6–8

for the pastry:
175g/6oz plain flour, sifted
½ teaspoon caster sugar
75g/3oz butter
2–3 tablespoons iced water

for the filling:
300ml/½pt single cream
petals of 8 marigolds
3 egg yolks
50g/2oz caster sugar
1 egg white, stiffly beaten

Pastry:
Place the flour and sugar in a bowl, add the butter and rub in until the mixture resembles fine breadcrumbs. Add enough iced water to mix to a firm dough. Wrap in clingfilm and chill in the refrigerator for about 30 minutes. Roll out the dough on a lightly floured surface and line a 20cm/8" flan tin. Prick all over with a fork, line with crumpled foil weighed down with beans and bake in a preheated oven 190C/375F/gas mark 5 for 8 minutes. Remove the pastry case and reduce the oven heat to 180C/350F/gas mark 4.

Filling:
Heat the cream slowly with the marigold petals. When hot, but not boiling, remove from the heat and stand, covered, for 10 minutes. Beat the egg yolks with the sugar, reheat the cream and pour through a strainer onto the eggs, beating well. Fold in the stiffly beaten egg white and pour the mixture into the pastry case. Bake for 20 minutes, until puffy and golden brown. Serve as soon as possible, scattered with a few marigold petals.

MARJORAM

History

Like so many herbs, the origins of marjoram are in Greece. There, its close relation, oregano (wild marjoram), covers the hillsides in glorious abundance in summer, filling the air with fragrance. Marjoram was introduced into this country in the Middle Ages, where ladies used it to perfume their baths and put into nosegays. The leaves were rubbed into floors and furniture to give them a pleasant fragrance. Marjoram has long been considered a herb of happiness, as well as of sweet fragrance. Bridal couples used to be crowned with garlands of marjoram and the herbalist Gerrard recommended the herb to those people who were given to 'over much sighing'. On heavy, hot, thundery days, marjoram used to be added to pails of fresh milk in the belief that it would preserve their sweetness.

Cultivation

Hardy herbaceous perennial, maximum growing height 60cm/2ft.
Marjoram is an easy plant to grow. It prefers full sun and like most Mediterranean plants, a well-drained soil. What you do need to do with marjoram is to use it regularly. Like so many herbs, it will turn woody and unattractive if not regularly cut back. Marjoram can be grown indoors – I have a pot, which sits in the kitchen above the dog beds, in the fond belief that it wards off doggy smells.

Preserving

You can freeze or dry the leaves, they are also good in oil or vinegar. As well as making an excellent tea, the leaves can be added to meat dishes and pasta and the French often use marjoram as an ingredient in bouquet garni. If you lay marjoram stems on a barbecue just before cooking, the smell is sufficiently strong to give your barbecued meats or fish a delicate marjoram flavour.

Stuffed Marrow with Tomato Sauce

Serves 4–6

1 large marrow

for stuffing
110g/4oz long grain rice
1 onion
40g/1½oz butter
1 cup of fresh marjoram
½ cup fresh mint
salt and pepper

For tomato sauce
1 onion
1 clove garlic
1 x 400g/14oz tin tomatoes
a little oil
salt and pepper
teaspoon of sugar
½ cup chopped basil

Peel the marrow, cut it in half, horizontally, and scoop out soft interior. Sprinkle with salt and leave to drain upside down for 30 minutes.

To make the stuffing, cook rice until tender. Melt the butter in a frying pan, chop and cook onion, add salt and pepper, herbs and cooked rice.

To make the sauce, cook chopped onion in a little oil, then add garlic, followed by tomatoes, sugar, salt and pepper. Bring to the boil and then add basil.

Pile stuffing into one side of the drained marrow and put the other half back on top. Place on an oiled piece of foil and pour a third of the tomato sauce over the length of the marrow. Seal the tin foil round the length of the marrow and bake in an ovenproof dish for one hour at 190C/375F/gas mark 5. Slice vertically and serve with remaining sauce.

MINT

History

According to Greek mythology Pluto loved a nymph called Minthe. However, his jealous wife flew into a rage and Pluto transformed Minthe into the herb mint. Everyone seems to have recognised the value of mint. The Pharisees used it as currency, it is mentioned by the Roman poet, Ovid, and by the herbalist Gerrard in 1597 and by Culpepper who clearly saw it as an aphrodisiac: 'The juice of garden mint taken in vinegar, stays bleeding and stirs up venery, or bodily lust'. The Romans used mint to flavour wines and sauces and it was so regarded as a herb, that in Italian churches you can find references to it where it was known as 'Erba Santa Maria'.

Cultivation

Hardy herbaceous perennial, maximum growing height 1m/3ft.

Mint likes somewhere moist and partially out of the sun. What I have found over the years is that you can usually plant mint in that part of the garden where you cannot grow anything else and once established it will flourish, often more than you would like. Many people plant mint in a large bucket in the ground to avoid the roots spreading and this is a sensible practice. Having said that, this is a herb I just love and I personally do not mind when it romps across the garden. If you plant mint near roses it will deter aphids.

Preserving

You can dry or freeze mint leaves. If you freeze them, we have found it best to freeze the stem with the leaves on it, in polythene bags, and then crush up the mint while still frozen when you take it out. Mint tea, which can be made from dried or fresh leaves, has long held a reputation for easing the symptoms of colds and flu and traditionally, in addition to mint sauce, mint leaves are added when cooking new potatoes or peas, put in salads, drinks and punches, soups and stuffings.

Lamb and Fresh Mint Curry

Serves 4

700g/1½lb boned lamb, preferably shoulder
(cut into 2.5cm/1in cubes with most of fat removed)
3 large onions, sliced
1 teaspoon salt
¼–½ teaspoon cayenne pepper
2.5cm/1in cube fresh ginger, peeled and chopped
2 garlic cloves, crushed
½ teaspoon turmeric
4 whole cardamom pods
2.5cm/1in stick cinnamon
4 whole cloves
3 tablespoons vegetable oil
2 tablespoons coriander leaves
3 tablespoons mint leaves
1 fresh green chilli
2 tablespoons lemon juice

Heat the oil in a heavy saucepan and brown the meat. Remove from the pan with a slotted spoon and put aside. Next, fry the onions until they begin to brown. Put the cinnamon stick, cardamom pods and cloves into the hot oil and stir them for about 5 seconds over medium-high heat. Return the meat and the onions to the pan. Add the salt, cayenne, ginger, garlic and turmeric and 2 cups of water. Bring to a simmer, cover, lower the heat and cook gently for 2–3 hours (adding more water if necessary). Blend the mint, coriander, chilli and lemon juice in a food processor until smooth. When meat is tender, add the blended mint and coriander mixture and simmer for the last few minutes.

MINT

There are many varieties of mint; here are the main ones:

Apple Mint
This is my favourite. It has large round hairy leaves which smell of mint and apple and it is a big plant, growing to over 1m/3ft if not regularly pruned.

Black Peppermint
The leaves of this plant are dark green. This is a very hardy plant and grows to a height of 75cm/2.5ft. It has a strong peppermint scent.

Corsican Mint
This is the baby of the family, growing to a height of just over 25mm/1in. It has tiny peppermint scented green leaves and pink flowers.

Eau de Cologne Mint
Smooth bergamot scented purple and green leaves with purple stems. It grows to a height of about 45cm/18in. It is not so useful as a culinary herb but looks very attractive in a garden.

Garden Mint
This is the most common mint. It can grow to a height of about 75cm/2.5ft. The leaves are small and hardy and it has a strong sharp flavour, ideal for mint sauce.

Ginger Mint
Smooth leaved mint, green with gold splashes on the leaves with a spicy flavour. It grows to a height of about 40cm/16in. This is a plant, which particularly needs pruning to maintain its golden growth.

Lemon Mint
Smooth delicate leaves with a strong lemon scent. A small plant, it grows to a maximum of 40cm/16in.

Moroccan Mint
Small bright green leaves, this plant grows to about 60cm/2ft. The taste is of sharp clean spearmint.

Pineapple Mint
This is another favourite with me. The plant smells quite extraordinarily like pineapple, with just an added touch of minty sharpness. It has pretty cream and green leaves and will grow to at least 60cm/2ft.

Tabbouleh

Serves 4

110g/4oz bulghar wheat
6 tablespoons (90ml) extra virgin olive oil
Juice of 1 small lemon
1 garlic clove, peeled and crushed
½ cucumber, peeled, deseeded and diced
2 ripe tomatoes, skinned (optional) and diced
4 tablespoons chopped fresh parsley
3 tablespoons chopped fresh mint
Salt and freshly ground black pepper
mint sprigs to garnish

Put the bulghar wheat into a bowl, add plenty of cold water to cover and leave to soak for 30 minutes. Meanwhile, put the olive oil, lemon juice and garlic in a small bowl, stir to mix and set aside until required.

Drain the bulghar wheat thoroughly, shaking off as much excess liquid as possible. Place in a bowl with the diced cucumber, diced tomatoes, spring onions and herbs.

Pour in the olive oil mixture and toss well. Season with salt and pepper to taste. Cover and leave to infuse for several hours or overnight until ready to serve. Garnish with mint sprigs.

MYRTLE

History

Myrtle is the stuff of legend. Venus was wearing a myrtle wreath when Paris gave her the golden apple. As a result, myrtle was planted around all the temples dedicated to her. It is said that one of Venus's favourite priestesses, by the name of Myrrha, was having trouble with a persistent suitor and so Venus turned her into myrtle to protect her. Because of myrtle's link with Venus, the herb is always associated with love and was woven into bridle wreaths. The Romans too, used it at weddings, feasts and celebrations. One of the Arabian stories tells of Adam banished from paradise, taking with him a sprig of myrtle from the place where he declared his love for Eve.

Cultivation

Half-hardy evergreen shrub, maximum growing height 3m/10ft.
As I know to my cost, myrtle does not like wind. It must have a sheltered place to thrive and prefers the full sun, and a well-drained soil. It grows very well in pots so you could stand it outside in summer and bring it inside in Winter. It really should not be in a temperature much less than 5C/41F.

Preserving

You can dry the leaves, the flowers and buds of myrtle and, of course, fresh leaves can be picked all the year round. For stronger smelling leaves pick them when the myrtle is in flower. The berries, once dried, can be ground up and used as a spice rather like a juniper berry. You can lay young branches of myrtle on lamb or pork, either in the oven or on the barbecue, for a delicious delicate flavour. Both flower and leaf can be used for pot pourri. Tea made from either dry or fresh leaves is said to be good for psoriasis and sinusitis. Myrtle is a beautiful delicate plant, which rightly has been admired for thousands of years.

Venison Casserole

Serves 4

900g/2lb venison, cut into 2.5cm/1in cubes
flour
3 Spanish onions, finely chopped
2 tablespoons vegetable oil
225g/8oz unsmoked bacon, diced
6 cloves garlic
3 sprigs myrtle
3 cloves
1 sprig each of marjoram, rosemary and thyme
½ bottle red wine
3 large carrots, quartered
3 medium potatoes, quartered
salt and freshly ground black pepper

Roll the venison cubes in seasoned flour. Heat the oil in a large heatproof casserole and fry the onions until soft. Remove from the pan and reserve. Fry the unsmoked bacon in the remaining fat until golden. Remove and reserve. Next add the venison cubes and fry until golden. Return the onions and bacon to the casserole. Add the garlic cloves, myrtle sprigs, cloves, marjoram, rosemary and thyme to the pan and simmer, covered, in a very low oven 150C/300F/gas mark 2 for 2 hours.

Reduce the wine over a high heat to half the original quantity and add to the stew with the quartered carrots and potatoes. Simmer for another hour.

OREGANO

History

The Ancient Greeks greatly revered the power of oregano to disinfect, to preserve and to heal. It was also popular with the Romans. Today we tend to associate it with Greece although it is now a native, not only of the Mediterranean, but also right across Europe into Asia, North Africa and North America, too.

Cultivation

Hardy herbaceous perennial, maximum growing height 60cm/2ft.
Like marjoram, oregano is fairly easy going about where it likes to be. It prefers full sun, but semi-shade will do, and preferably a well drained soil. It will grow indoors and is one of those herbs, which do very well in pots – outside in summer, inside in winter.

Preserving

With leaves readily available for most of the year, you will only need to preserve oregano in the very middle of winter. The leaves can be frozen or dried, placed in oil or vinegar. If you are thinking of preserving in oil or vinegar, drying the flower heads makes a very attractive and fragrant addition to a bottle of either. Oregano is reputed to have properties of comfort. It relieves symptoms of nervousness, headaches, depression and helps promote sleep. A sleep pillow stuffed with dry oregano is very helpful. A tea made from dried or fresh oregano leaves will ease coughs, gall bladder problems, stomach disorders and general exhaustion. It is also very helpful in the prevention of seasickness. If you have a toothache, chew fresh oregano leaves and it will temporarily relieve it, though not enough to let you off a trip to the dentist!

As a culinary herb, oregano blends very well with garlic and/or chilli. Add to pastas, pizzas or any egg or cheese dish – good, too, with fish.

Beef Provencal

Serves 4

700g/1½1b stewing steak
2 leeks sliced
2 cloves of garlic, crushed
1 cup of fresh oregano
1 x 400g tin of tomatoes
2 bay leaves
1 cup of water
1 beef stock cube
1½ glasses of red wine
450g/1lb baby potatoes
4 small courgettes sliced
12 black olives
1 tablespoon flour

Heat a little oil in a large saucepan or flameproof casserole dish. Add steak cut into bite-sized cubes. Fry until browned all over and then remove from pan. Add leeks and garlic to pan, and then fry until a light golden brown.

Stir in tomatoes, bay leaves, oregano, water, crumbled stock cube, wine, potatoes and return the steak. Bring to the boil, reduce heat, cover and simmer for 40 minutes or until steak is tender. (The dish may be cooked in the oven, in which case reduce cooking time to about 25 minutes at 160C/325F/gas mark 3).

Then add courgettes and olives and cook fast for another 10 minutes. Blend flour with a little water and stir into mixture. Leave on the heat, stirring regularly for a few minutes until mixture boils and thickens.

This dish is a meal in itself, a staple diet in many French farmhouses. Serve with French bread to mop up the sauce!

PARSLEY

History

Parsley was grown in the herb gardens of the Emperor Charlemagne in the 8th century. It was well known in medieval England and then taken to America by early settlers. Parsley seeds sprinkled into the hair were thought to be a cure for baldness. Greek warriors fed parsley to their chariot horses. It is said that if the mistress of the house sows the parsley, it always flourishes and so will she. Where the parsley thrives 'the missus is master' goes a saying from Devon.

Cultivation

Hardy bi-annual, maximum growing height 38cm/15in.
Parsley is easy to grow provided it is kept in a rich moist soil and has at least some sunshine during the day. There are two main types of parsley, the more familiar curled parsley and the flat leaf French parsley. Curled, without doubt, is easier to grow and better at coping with wind and rain. Equally without doubt, French parsley has a far better and stronger flavour. As far as I am concerned, I use curled parsley for decoration but flat leaf parsley in cooking. Parsley is only a bi-annual and should be dug up at the end of the second year and re-sown. Leaves tend to be of a better quality in the first year than the second.

Preserving

You can dry or freeze parsley (both types) but again this a herb I would recommend you freeze 'whole', the stem and the leaves together and then simply break them up while still frozen. I do not think much of dried parsley. I feel it loses much of the delicate flavour and ends up looking like grass mowings, if you are lucky in retaining the colour, or sawdust if you are not! Raw leaves can be added to salads, you can sprinkle chopped parsley over egg dishes, soups, fish, boiled potatoes, mayonnaise.... any number of things. It is recognised that parsley is a good thing to chew to freshen the breath, and certainly it is recommended after eating garlic.

Pasta with Prawns

Serves 4–6

225g/8oz prawns (frozen are fine)
110g/4oz mushrooms
1 onion
1 x 400g/14oz tin tomatoes
2 cloves of garlic
150ml/¼pt dry white wine
salt and pepper
400g/14oz pasta shells
1 cup fresh parsley

Heat a little olive oil in a large frying pan. Peel and chop onion, and cook in oil for about 5 minutes until soft but not brown. Add peeled and chopped garlic. Then add half the parsley, and the prawns and mushrooms. Cook on a gentle heat, stirring continuously. Add salt and pepper and the tin of tomatoes. After 2–3 minutes, add wine and simmer gently for another 3 minutes.

Meanwhile, cook the pasta in a large pan of boiling salt water, according to packet instructions. Drain pasta and transfer to a large warm serving bowl, add remaining parsley and a little oil. Toss lightly and then add contents of frying pan. Toss again and serve immediately with French bread and a green salad.

ROSEMARY

History

Rosemary was mentioned in the Anglo-Saxon herbal *The Leech Book of Bald* in the tenth century, and Tudor England grew it in pots, and against walls and used it in topiary. The wood was once used to make lutes and other musical instruments. Rosemary is the herb of remembrance and Greek scholars wore it on their heads to help them retain information. It has been carried at weddings to represent fidelity. There is a legend that rosemary flowers are blue because it was one of the bushes that sheltered the Holy Family on their flight into Egypt. Mary laid her cloak over the white flowers on the bushes and they have been blue ever since.

Cultivation

Hardy evergreen perennial, maximum growing height 1–2m/3–6ft.
Up on our windy cliff at Halzephron we have tried to winter numerous herbs outside. There are really only two herbs that can survive – one is the curry plant and the other, strangely enough, is that plant so associated with the warm Mediterranean – rosemary. Place your rosemary plants close together so that they form a bush or hedge and they seem almost indestructible. Our various clumps of rosemary are constantly in use and cropped very hard at times, yet they bounce back and in fact seem to thrive on it. Rosemary does need a well-drained soil.

Preserving

You cannot freeze rosemary but it dries extremely well. Dry it on the branch, bunching the branches together and hanging them downwards, then strip off the leaves, when dry, and store in an airtight jar. Fresh branches of rosemary in a room are lovely. It is ideal for pot pourri and you can lay sprigs of rosemary among your sheets and towels. If you place plenty of rosemary stems on the barbecue, not only will your meat or fish taste delicious the aroma also discourages insects. A rosemary tea is good for aches and pains and you can use it as an antiseptic gargle.

Navarin of Lamb

Serves 4–6

6 lamb noisettes
1 onion, chopped
3 cloves of garlic
1 cup of fresh rosemary
⅓ cup plain flour
4 cups (1 litre) water
½ glass red wine
2 chicken stock cubes
2 tablespoons of tomato paste
110g/4oz green beans
2 sticks of celery
110g/4oz baby carrots

Heat a little olive oil in a frying pan. Add noisettes and fry on both sides until brown. Remove the meat from the pan. Add onions and garlic. Stir over the heat until lightly browned and then add flour, stirring in continuously until mixture is smooth and brown. Then stir in water, crumbled stock cubes, wine, tomato paste and rosemary stirring continuously over the heat until mixture boils and thickens. Then simmer for 5 minutes.

Top and tail beans and cut into short lengths. Cut celery into short lengths and prepare carrots.

Then combine noisettes, vegetables and the sauce into a casserole dish and bake in a moderate oven 180C/350F/gas mark 4 for 1½ hours.

SAGE

History

Sage was introduced into Britain by the Romans and was by all accounts the most popular of culinary and medicinal herbs in medieval times. Throughout history, sage has been renowned for its powers of long levity, '...why should a man die when sage grows in his garden'. Perhaps as a spin off from its association with long life, sage is said to ease grief. For this reason in seventeenth century England, it was often planted on graves.

Cultivation

Hardy evergreen shrub, maximum growing height 75cm/2.5ft.
Sage prefers full sunlight and a well-drained soil but is a reasonably hardy plant. There are a variety of different sages in addition to the broadleaf sage most commonly seen in this country. There is purple sage which is ideal for teas, tri-colour sage that is very hardy and has very attractive pink and white leaves, there is variegated sage and variegated purple sage, both with attractive leaf markings. There is also pineapple sage, which is not very hardy, but has delightful scarlet flowers and a strong pineapple flavour. Sage needs to be cut back after flowering in order to keep it bushy and healthy. Left to its own devices it will become woody and straggly and look most unattractive. You can put two or three sages of different colours together in a bed, to great effect.

Preserving

You cannot really freeze sage very successfully. Dry the leaves slowly to preserve flavour and colour, as there is a tendency for them to become musty. Sage vinegar is very good and fresh young sage leaves can be scattered in salad as well as their more traditional use for poultry stuffing. Sage is a great deodoriser – a pan of boiling sage will take away all cooking and animal smells. As well as promoting a long life, sage aids digestion, helps combat diarrhoea and is well known for easing menopausal sweating.

Chicken Breasts with Sage

Serves 4–6

6 skinless chicken breasts
seasoned flour
1 tablespoon olive oil
1 tablespoon butter
50g/2oz thin gammon rashers
150ml/¼pt dry white wine
150ml/¼pt chicken stock
12 sage leaves
salt and freshly ground black pepper

Cut each breast in half, lengthways and coat with seasoned flour. Heat the oil and butter in a sauté pan and lightly brown the chicken. Cut the gammon into narrow strips and add to the chicken. When the chicken is golden brown, pour in the wine and enough stock to cover about two-thirds of the chicken breasts. Add the roughly chopped sage. Cover the pan and simmer for 15–20 minutes. Remove to a serving dish and keep warm. Increase the heat and rapidly boil the liquid until it has reduced to a thin coating consistency. Season to taste with salt and pepper. Pour the sauce over the chicken fillets and serve at once.

SORREL

History

Sorrel is a herb, which is rather underrated by everyone except the French, who, among other things, make the most delicious sorrel soup. There appear to be no links between sorrel and the ancient civilisations. The earliest reference I can find is Culpepper who describes it as a herb, which '...quenches thirst and procures an appetite in fainting or decaying stomachs'. Certainly sorrel has a reputation for quenching thirsts and country people frequently used to pick sorrel from the hedgerows when thirsty during haymaking on hot summer days.

Cultivation

Hardy perennial, maximum growing height 1.2m/4ft.
Sorrel likes the sun and a relatively rich and moist soil. The leaves are best gathered when they are young and if you cover sorrel plants with cloches during the winter, you should continue to have leaf production. Alternatively you can grow sorrel indoors in pots and your plant should last for anything up to five years before needing to be replaced or divided up to promote new growth.

Preserving

Dried sorrel does not work – it loses its flavour and colour – it is best to freeze sorrel and it freezes very well. You can chop young leaves into a salad and sorrel is lovely too in salad dressing. You can cook sorrel as you would spinach, or introduce it into soups, casseroles, omelettes and in sauces for fish, poultry or red meat. A tea from sorrel leaves – which need to be fresh and young – is good for treating kidney and liver ailments. You will find many culinary uses for the sharp, slightly acidic, flavour of sorrel. It is a splendid herb in the kitchen.

Salmon Fillets with Sorrel

Serves 4

4 salmon fillets
150ml/¼pt fish stock
9 tablespoons dry white wine
2 shallots, finely chopped
425ml/¾pt double cream
75g/3oz sorrel, ribs removed,
washed and large leaves torn into 2–3 pieces
40g/1½oz butter
1 tablespoon lemon juice
oil for frying
salt and freshly ground black pepper

Put the fish stock, white wine and shallots into a sauté pan. Place over a high heat and reduce until the liquid becomes syrupy. Add the double cream, bring to the boil and cook until the sauce thickens slightly. Toss in the sorrel. After 25 seconds, remove the pan from the heat and swirl in the butter, cut into small knobs, by shaking the pan. Do not use a whisk as this would tear the sorrel leaves. Add the lemon juice, salt and pepper. Heat a large frying pan and add a little oil. Season the salmon fillets with salt and pepper and fry for approximately 5 minutes on each side until just cooked through. Remove from the pan and serve immediately, coated with the sorrel sauce.

SWEET CICELY

History

The botanical name for this lovely plant is the Greek name for perfume. It has been in Europe for many centuries and a similar sister plant grows in North America. The green leaves of sweet cicely, which are fern like, give off a myrrh type of scent with just a touch of aniseed. Perhaps sweet cicely's most famous claim to fame is that the ripe seeds are used to flavour the liqueur, Chartreuse.

Cultivation

Hardy herbaceous perennial, maximum growing height 1m/3ft.
Sweet cicely prefers a little shade for part of the day and a rich soil. The whole of the sweet cicely plant has value, including the root. Although this is a perennial, every two years or so it would be a good idea to dig up and start again, using the root as described below.

Preserving

Each part of sweet cicely can be preserved as follows:
Seed – pick unripe seeds when green, which have a lovely sweet flavour, and toss them into fruit salads or ice-cream instead of sugar. Use ripe seeds, which are ripe when they turn brown, in cooked dishes such as fruit pies or crumbles, either whole or crushed.
Leaf – pick young leaves and chop finely in soups and stews, salad dressings, omelettes and vegetables. If you are cooking acidic foods, such as gooseberries, rhubarb or currants, cook with some sweet cicely leaves and this will reduce the acidity and the amount of sugar you will need to add to the dish.
Root – peel, chop and serve raw with salad dressing, or cook as a root vegetable and serve with butter. You can steep the cleaned and peeled root in an infusion of wine or brandy, which is considered to be a tonic, particularly useful for teenagers or the elderly.
An important point with sweet cicely – it is a marvellous aid to the diabetic for it provides a completely harmless sweetener to a whole range of dishes.

Rhubarb Compote with Sweet Cicely

Serves 4–6

700g/1½lb rhubarb, trimmed and cut into pieces
225g/8oz caster sugar
2 tablespoons sweet cicely leaves, chopped

Preheat oven to 200C/400F/gas mark 6. Put the rhubarb into a roasting pan and top with the sugar. Sprinkle over the chopped sweet cicely. Cover the tin with foil and seal well. Cook in the oven for 20 minutes, then remove, but leave the foil in place for a further 10 minutes. Serve hot, or leave to cool and eat later.

TARRAGON

History

We produce a tarragon dip called 'Little Dragon' because Dracunculus is the Latin name given to this herb, meaning just that. It probably derives the name from its distinct, almost fiery, tang and it also has a reputation for curing the bites of venomous creatures. The Moors, who conquered Spain, probably introduced tarragon into Europe but outside Spain it remained undiscovered by the rest of Europe until the mid sixteenth century. '... Tis highly cordial and friend to head, heart and liver.' –.John Evelyn 1699. Today, tarragon is best known as a culinary herb.

Cultivation

Hardy perennial, maximum growing height 1m/3ft.

Tarragon needs a sunny and sheltered spot and is another herb which does not like wet feet – ideally, therefore, a rich soil but light and dry if possible. There are two types of tarragon – French tarragon and Russian tarragon. French tarragon produces no flowers so the only way to propagate this plant is to divide the roots every spring, just before the growing season. Russian tarragon, on the other hand, does produce seeds. It is generally believed, and I would agree with this, that Russian tarragon is really not worth growing for it is French tarragon, which has all the flavour. If you are offered tarragon seeds, you know it is the inferior herb you will be buying. Tarragon is susceptible to frost, cold and damp generally, so in winter either bring it indoors or protect it with a mulch, having cut it right back in the autumn.

Preserving

You can freeze or dry tarragon or infuse the leaves in oil or vinegar. Tarragon is one of the *fines herbes* and is used in the making of all the great sauces – i.e. Béarnaise, tartar and hollandaise sauces. Add tarragon leaves to mayonnaise, salad dressings, omelettes, to any red meats or vegetables. Tarragon is particularly associated with chicken and is delicious in a stuffing or chicken casserole. Quite honestly, I do not think a herb garden can be complete without tarragon.

Pork fillets with Tarragon

Serves 4

6 sprigs of tarragon
300ml/¼pt double cream
40g/1½oz butter
4 pork fillets
juice of half a lemon
salt and black pepper

Strip about 12 leaves from the tarragon sprigs. Heat the cream in a small pan with the remaining tarragon leaves, bringing slowly to boiling point. Put on one side, cover and leave for about 20 minutes to infuse.

Melt the butter in a frying pan, cook the fillets quickly. Then remove and keep hot. Pour the cream through a strainer into the frying pan and stir well to mix with the juices. Add juice of half a lemon and plenty of salt and black pepper. Pour over the fillets and scatter the reserved tarragon leaves.

Serve with new potatoes or rice and a green salad.

(This recipe works equally well with veal or chicken breasts)

THYME

History

The Egyptians used thyme to embalm their dead. Thyme tea is said to be good for hangovers! Since ancient Greece, thyme has been a symbol of courage. Lancastrian ladies, during the period of the War of the Roses, embroidered a bee hovering over thyme on the corners of scarves, which were given to their knight to wear in battle or tournaments. An old Greek legend claimed thyme sprang from the tears of Helen of Troy. Rudyard Kipling described the scent of thyme on the Sussex downs as 'like dawn in Paradise'.

Cultivation

Evergreen shrub, maximum growing height 38cm/15in.
Thyme likes full sun and a well-drained soil. Once again think of scorched Mediterranean hillsides and you can see why thyme has no liking for damp English clay. Thyme grows beautifully in pots and you might consider this the best way to maintain your supply. Having said that, with so many different varieties of thyme available you can make the most delightful and colourful bed of different types of thyme. If you are leaving your plants outside then a good mulch in winter will help – certainly we have a number of beds of thyme, which have come through winter gales and storms without any problem, year after year.

Preserving

You cannot freeze thyme, drying is far better and thyme is another herb, which is excellent to use in oil or vinegar. The leaf, dried or fresh, is excellent in marinades, stuffings, sauces, soups and casseroles, with meats, poultry and fish. The ultimate luxury – if you fancy your chances as a bee-keeper, planting bushes of thyme around a hive will result in thyme honey which is one of the most highly praised of all honeys.

Pork Cassoulet

Serves 4–6

350g/12oz lima beans (or equivalent)
6 pork medallions
350g/12oz sausages – either continental or thick pork
4 bacon rashers chopped
3 large onions
1 x 400g/14oz tin tomatoes
2 tablespoons of tomato paste
2 bay leaves
4 cloves of garlic (crushed)
2 vegetable stock cubes
2 cups of water
1 cup of fresh thyme

Soak beans overnight, drain and then cook beans in a large saucepan of boiling water for about an hour, until tender. Drain, combine beans, crumbled stock cubes, water, tinned tomatoes, tomato paste and bay leaves in a saucepan. Bring to the boil, cover and then simmer for 30 minutes.

Heat a little olive oil in a frying pan and add onions and bacon, followed by pork medallions and sausages. Fry until meat is browned on both sides. Then add the thyme and combine with the bean mixture in a casserole dish and bake in a moderate oven 180C/350F/gas mark 4 for 1½ hours.

Serve with French bread.

THYME

There is a wide variety of thyme – these are the most readily available:

Common Thyme
This is the thyme you will mostly see selling in garden centres. It is aromatic, hardy, with pointed oval mid green leaves and pale lilac flowers.

English Wild Thyme
This is very hardy. It is a creeper, which gives good ground cover and has mauve flowers. The leaves, however, are only mildly scented.

Broad Leaf Thyme
This is a good plant to have if you use a lot of thyme. The leaves are very strongly flavoured and larger and rounder than common thyme. The shrub becomes quite bushy and produces pink-mauve flowers.

Golden Creeping Thyme
This is a lovely little plant with golden leaves and rose purple flowers. However it does need full sunshine as otherwise the leaves lose their colour.

Woolly Thyme
A tiny creeping thyme, this one has very hairy grey leaves and a pink flower and grows only to a height of three inches.

Doone Valley Thyme
Another creeper with bright green leaves with gold splashes on them and pale purple flowers. It is slightly lemon scented and a very pretty plant.

Silver Lemon Queen
Delightful silver splashed leaves, pale pink flowers and a slightly lemony flavour to the leaves.

Minus Thyme
Probably the tiniest of the thyme, this is a creeper with pink flowers and tiny green leaves. Grows to a height of about two inches.

Golden Lemon Creeping Thyme
A creeper with pink flowers and golden lemon leaves, very attractive to look at but not a particularly strong scent.

Herba-Barona
This herb has arching branches, rose coloured flowers and dark green leaves, and it is most attractive. The scent is that of caraway.

Marinated Goats' Cheese with Thyme

Serves 4–6

6–8 small fresh goats' cheeses
12 black peppercorns
12 green peppercorns
1 bay leaf, crumbled
6 sprigs thyme
Olive oil

Pack the cheeses into a wide-mouthed glass jar, scattering the peppercorns, crumbled bay leaf and thyme sprigs amongst them. Top up the jar with enough olive oil to cover the cheeses and seal tightly.

Allow at least two weeks before opening. The cheeses may be left for longer, stored in a cool place, but they will grow stronger the longer they are kept.

Serve with biscuits or fresh-baked bread, or grill gently and serve on a bed of mixed salad leaves.

WINTER SAVORY

History

Winter savory is one of the oldest herbs used for flavouring. The Romans were mad about it. Virgil describes it in a poem about country life. Winter savory had made its way to North America by 1672 and Culpepper describes it as 'a good remedy for the colic and iliac passion'. It has a spiciness, almost a pepper taste to it, and as well as being considered a stimulant, it has always been awarded the properties of an aphrodisiac. Branches of winter savory used to be put on household open fires to disinfect the house. It was a method used for centuries.

Cultivation

Hardy evergreen shrub, maximum growing height 38cm/15in.
Winter savory prefers full sun and a well-drained soil, but it is a fairly easygoing plant and attractive too, with tiny pink and white flowers. The leaves give it an appearance not dissimilar to rosemary. This is a plant which benefits from gentle and regular pruning and will need some protection in winter. Failure to prune will create some unattractive woody growth.

Preserving

The leaves do not freeze, but dry very well or can be added to vinegar or oil. The dried leaves are very good chopped and sprinkled on food if you need a salt free diet. Traditionally, dried savory is used in the making of salami. The fresh or dried flowering top of the savory can be used as a tea, which is said will stimulate the appetite and ease indigestion or wind. A rather jolly tonic can be recommended by adding sprigs of fresh winter savory to wine and drinking regularly, particularly after a fever (sounds good to me!). The odd branch of savory in your bath is not only fragrant, but an antiseptic as well.

Gratin of Fennel

Serves 4

4 bulbs Florence fennel
6 tablespoons olive oil
1 medium onion, sliced
2 cloves garlic, sliced
400g/14oz tomatoes (skinned, deseeded and chopped)
1 tablespoon winter savory, chopped
salt and freshly ground black pepper
1 glass dry white wine
5 tablespoons coarse dried breadcrumbs
2 tablespoons grated Parmesan cheese

Remove the outer leaves of the fennel and slice the bulbs thickly. Heat 4 tablespoons of the olive oil and gently sauté the onion and garlic. Add the fennel and let the pieces colour slightly, turning from time to time. Heat the oven to 200C/400F/gas mark 6. Add the tomatoes and herbs, season with salt and pepper and simmer for 5 minutes. Transfer all the vegetables to a gratin dish. Deglaze the pan with the wine over a high heat then pour the wine over the fennel. Mix the breadcrumbs with the Parmesan cheese and scatter over the top. Drizzle over the remaining oil and bake for 20 minutes or until golden brown.

PRESERVING HERBS

There are three ways in which to preserve herbs:
>   Dry them.
>   Freeze them.
>   Preserve them in oil or vinegar.

Whichever method you use, the way in which you harvest your herbs is very important. Always collect them in the morning, after the dew has evaporated. This is the time of day when photosynthesis is under way and essential oils are concentrated in the leaves for maximum potency and flavour. Avoid a wet day. Choose young fresh parts of the plant and handle them carefully. It is very easy to cause bruising if you are not careful. As a general rule, leaves are at their sweetest before the plant flowers, and roots should only be harvested after flowering. Whatever method of preserving you intend to use, start work as soon as the herbs are picked. Deterioration begins the moment the herbs leave the living plant so it is important to move quickly.

Drying

Drying is a slow process. There is absolutely no shortcut. You cannot dry your herbs in the oven as the water within the plant will evaporate too quickly and the essential oils will be completely lost. In theory you can use the microwave, but again there is a very high risk of destroying the properties of the plant in the process. Drying them naturally is really the only sensible way. Once dried, herbs should be stored in dark glass with an airtight stopper, away from sunlight, moisture and dust. Avoid plastic or metal containers as they can affect the chemistry of the herb.

Drying leaves

Wipe off any soil but try to avoid washing the leaf. Either lay individual leaves on a tray covered in brown paper or hang the leaves by their stems. The ideal place to dry leaves is in an airing cupboard or warm loft and an ideal drying temperature is between 32–20C/90–80F. It is important air can circulate. Herbs with small leaves should either be dried flat or you will need to put a bag of muslin over the leaves to collect them if they fall away from the plant.

Drying Flowers

Dry flowers in exactly the same way as leaves. It is very important that you handle drying flowers carefully, particularly if you are going to break down the flowers into individual petals. It is so easy to damage them.

Drying Seeds and Fruit

Remove the seed heads and hang them to dry over a box, or a sheet of paper, or in a bag of fine muslin, so that as the seeds start to dry they fall somewhere they can be collected. Seeds dry very quickly, much quicker than leaves or flowers. So far as fruit is concerned, they will take longer and should be turned from time to time if drying them flat.

Drying Roots

All roots should be clean and fibrous parts removed before drying. Divide thick roots down the middle to create smaller pieces to speed up drying. Roots require a higher temperature 50C/120F is ideal.

Drying Bark

Bark may need washing to remove insects and moss, and then dry it slowly in a warm airy dark place, as flat as possible.

Freezing Herbs

Freezing is a good method because it ensures that colour and flavour are maintained, providing you freeze young leaves and freeze them quickly. The easiest way to freeze herbs is to simply put them whole, on the stem, into freezer bags. When you take them out to use them, crush and chop them while they are still frozen. This avoids them turning into mush. Another very handy way to freeze herbs is to chop the leaves finely and put them into ice-cube trays and top up with water. This means that when you come to use them you can just pop out as many ice-cubes as necessary, returning the rest to the freezer.

Preserving in Oil and Vinegar

This is a delicious way to preserve herbs. The resultant flavoured oils and vinegars can be used for dressings or marinades, in pickles and chutneys. Make sure the herbs are dry and simply put them into a bottle with perhaps a few peppercorns or spices of your choice. Fill up with oil or vinegar and seal. As an alternative to oil or vinegar, you can use alcohol. You can team together herbs and fruit, soak them in brandy, gin, whiskey or vodka with delicious results.

The Authors

Deborah Fowler was 17 when her first short story was published. Since then she has written over six hundred short stories, eight novels and a wide range of non-fiction. Deborah's second love is gardening and when she and her family moved to Cornwall ten years ago, the idea of a herb farm was born. Moving to such a beautiful part of the world, the Fowlers felt that they wanted to put something back and the idea of creating a business which provided employment, seemed the best way to achieve this. Halzephron Herb Farm now employs between eight and ten people, according to the season and has established a reputation country-wide for its range of culinary herb products.

Sally Cuckson spent the early 1970s cooking in chalets in order to pursue her passion for skiing. However, a broken leg and an increasing interest in producing good food soon established cooking as Sally's main enthusiasm. After the chalets, she worked for three years in a beach restaurant in St Tropez. In the early 1980s she moved onto charter yachts – her first was seventy-five feet long, but as her reputation grew so did the size of the yachts. The largest she ever worked on was two hundred and eighty-five feet! When she was chef on one of the larger yachts she used to do her shopping by helicopter, which has made Tescos seem a little tame ever since!

The Fowlers and the Cucksons are family friends and when the idea of Halzephron Herb Farm took shape, Sally was the obvious person to help develop the products. The recipes in this book aim to be as simple and straightforward as possible, Sally's philosophy being that if the recipes can be produced on board a yacht in a force nine gale, then they are probably just about suitable for the average domestic kitchen surrounded by the joys of family life.

Halzephron Herb Farm Shop

Halzephron Herb Farm Shop is perched on a cliff top with spectacular views overlooking Mounts Bay. The shop enjoys a considerable reputation for its range of culinary herb products. These include marinades, sauces, dips and preserves – the recipes of which have all been created by the authors of this book. Most of the culinary products are available for sampling. Halzephron Herb Farm also offers a wide range of medicinal herb products.

Directions

From Helston, take the A3083 towards the Lizard. As you pass RNAS Culdrose on the left, look out for a right hand turn to Gunwalloe. Take this little road and follow it through the village. Towards the end of the village, heading to Church Cove, you will pass the famous Halzephron Inn on your left. At this point look ahead of you up the road and you will see a white house standing alone on top of the cliff, which is the farm.

Opening Hours

From 1st March to 30th September, each year, Monday to Saturday inclusive 11am to 4pm. The shop is closed on Sundays, but is open for mail order all year round. Tel: 01326 240652 www.halzherb.com